WHALES

LIVING WILD

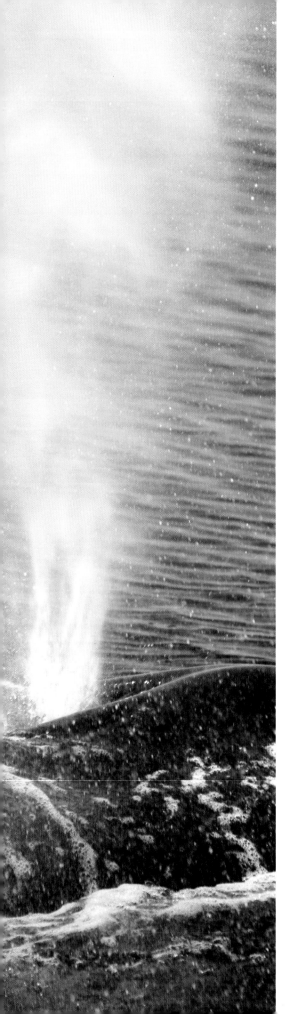

LIVING WILD

Published by Creative Paperbacks
P.O. Box 227, Mankato, Minnesota 56002
Creative Paperbacks is an imprint of The Creative Company
www.thecreativecompany.us

Design and production by Mary Herrmann
Art direction by Rita Marshall
Printed by Corporate Graphics in the United States of America

Photographs by 123rf (Hilma Anderson, Jaime Brum, Christopher Meder), Alamy (Peter Arnold, Inc., F. Bettex-Mysterra.org, Photos 12, Steve Bloom Images), Dreamstime (Brett Atklins, Bill Curtsinger, Rob Emery, Eric Isselee, Mandimiles, Melissaf84, Ken Moore, Ruth Peterkin, Victoria Purdie, Sburel), Getty Images (Buyenlarge, Brandon Cole, Rob Dalton, Hirova Minakuchi, Andy Newman/Florida Keys News Bureau, Flip Nicklin, Paul Nicklin, James Edwin McConnell, Yva Momatiuk & John Eastcott, Brian J. Skerry), iStockphoto (Marshall Bruce, Jan Dirk-Hansen, Marc Fowler, Jclegg, Jocrebbin, Rod Kaye, Earle Keatley, Nikontiger, Wolfgang Roll, Francisco Romero, Arne Thaysen, Elizabeth Tighe-Andino, Dale Walsh)

The Library of Congress has cataloged the hardcover edition as follows:
Gish, Melissa.
Whales / by Melissa Gish.
p. cm. — (Living wild)
Includes bibliographical references and index.
Summary: A look at whales, including their habitats, physical characteristics such as their streamlined bodies, behaviors, relationships with humans, and threatened status in the world today.
ISBN 978-1-60818-084-4 (hardcover)
ISBN 978-0-89812-676-1 (pbk)
1. Whales—Juvenile literature. I. Title.

QL737.C4G46 2011
599.5—dc22   2010028414

CPSIA: 061313 PO1705

9 8 7 6 5 4 3 2

WHALES

Melissa Gish

On a bright July morning off the coast of southeastern Alaska, a vast school of

herring scatters in the water of Lynn Canal.
Several humpback whales come into view.

On a bright July morning off the coast of southeastern Alaska, a vast school of herring scatters in the water of Lynn Canal. Several humpback whales come into view. The whales dive beneath the herring and begin emitting high-pitched calls, frightening the fish upward. Then they swim in a circle, blowing bubbles that rise to the surface and create a barrier through which the herring will not pass.

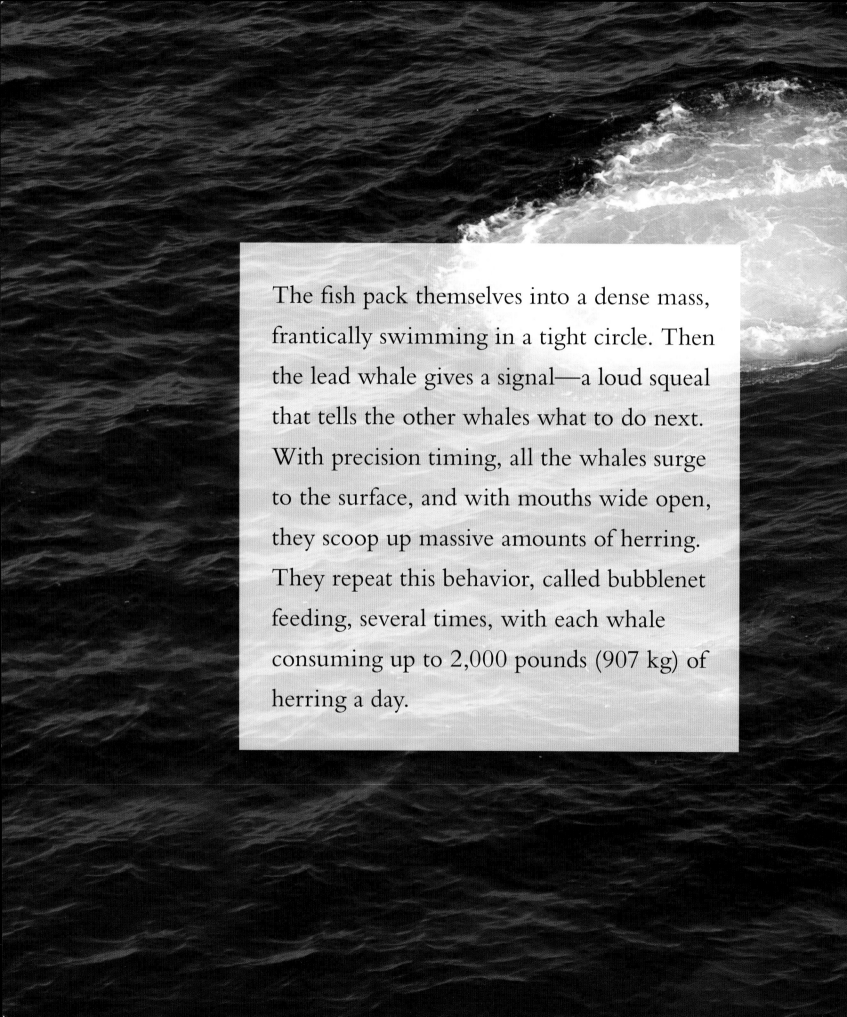

The fish pack themselves into a dense mass, frantically swimming in a tight circle. Then the lead whale gives a signal—a loud squeal that tells the other whales what to do next. With precision timing, all the whales surge to the surface, and with mouths wide open, they scoop up massive amounts of herring. They repeat this behavior, called bubblenet feeding, several times, with each whale consuming up to 2,000 pounds (907 kg) of herring a day.

WHERE IN THE WORLD THEY LIVE

■ **Humpback Whale**
worldwide

■ **Right Whale**
North Atlantic,
North Pacific,
Southern Ocean

■ **Beluga Whale**
Arctic and
sub-Arctic seas

■ **Fin Whale**
worldwide

■ **Minke Whale**
open seas
worldwide

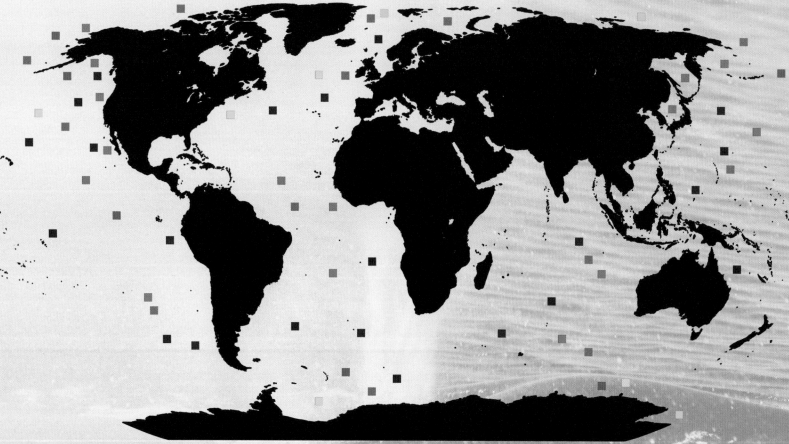

The nearly 40 species of whale are distributed throughout the world's oceans. Some range worldwide, some are found near certain coastlines, and others are rarely spotted in the open seas. The colored squares represent common locations of selected species found in the wild today.

■ **Sperm Whale**
worldwide—
including near poles

■ **Gray Whale**
Pacific Ocean

■ **Blue Whale**
worldwide—
concentrated in
northeast Pacific

WONDERFUL WHALES

W hales are among the largest creatures to inhabit Earth today. Their ancestors existed on the planet millions of years before humans appeared, and today's whales have survived despite the dangers of recent centuries, such as whale hunting and water pollution. Still, many species are either **extinct** or endangered, as in the case of the North Atlantic right whale, whose population has fallen below 350.

Whales belong to the Cetacea order of animals. This name is derived from the Latin *cetus*, which comes from a Greek word for an enormous sea creature. There are two kinds of cetaceans (*seh-TAY-shunz*): those with teeth, of the Odontoceti suborder, and those without teeth, of the suborder Mysticeti. Along with porpoises, dolphins, and killer whales, 25 whale species make up the Odontoceti. Thirteen species of non-toothed whale are called baleen whales. They are named for the baleen plates in their mouths that allow them to feed on many tiny sea creatures filtered from water.

Baleen was once called whalebone, but it is not made of bone. It is made of keratin, the same hard but flexible

People once feared whales and other large, unknown sea creatures and depicted them as monsters.

A blue whale's heart weighs about 1,300 pounds (590 kg), and its main blood vessel is so big that a human could crawl through it.

substance found in human fingernails. Shaped like combs with frayed edges, the baleen plates, located on a whale's upper and lower jaw, work like sieves. The whale scoops up a mouthful of water and then loosely closes its jaws. It then presses its tongue against the roof of its mouth to force out the water through its baleen plates, trapping tiny shrimp, fish, and drifting **plankton** inside its mouth. Whales with teeth—typically cold-water creatures—feed on larger prey, from fish and squid to seals, and sometimes even smaller whales.

Whales are found in every ocean on Earth. They vary greatly in size, with the smallest being the 9-foot-long (2.7 m) dwarf sperm whale and the largest being the blue whale, which can reach more than 100 feet (30 m) in length and is the largest animal on Earth. Most male whales are 20 to 30 percent larger than females. All whales have the same basic body shape—long and streamlined, which allows for little **resistance** as a whale cuts through the water, enabling it to dive and surface easily.

Whales, except the all-white beluga, are dark on top and light on the bottom. This type of **camouflage** is called countershading. When light shines on the whale from the

A whale's baleen plate grows continuously throughout its lifetime and eventually wears down along the edges.

Researchers in southeastern Alaska have identified about 1,900 individual humpback whales simply by studying and recording their tail markings.

top, it creates a shadow on its lighter underside and makes it less detectable from below. This helps whales to both avoid predators and capture prey. Except for humans, whales have few natural enemies. Larger toothed whales, such as sperm and killer whales, may hunt smaller whales—especially babies. Sharks are also a threat. Because sharks are drawn to the scent of blood in the water, a single shark attacking a whale usually leads to a gathering of sharks against which even the largest whales cannot defend.

The tails of whales and their relatives are unique among sea animals. At the end of the tail are two flat, boneless pads called flukes. The whale uses the muscles in its back and tail to wave the flukes up and down. This motion propels the whale forward—at speeds of up to 20 miles (32 km) per hour for blue whales. To help it steer as it swims, the whale uses its pectoral flippers. These are located on each side of the chest, below and behind the head. The flippers of all toothed whales have bones similar to those in a human's hand, enabling the whale to twist its pectoral flippers somewhat sideways in order to slow down or stop swimming. A whale uses the dorsal fin on its back to steady itself as it swims.

Humpbacks have the longest flippers of any whale, and part of their scientific name means "large wings."

Whales are marine mammals, meaning they live in the water and belong to a class of animals that, with the exceptions of the egg-laying platypus and hedgehog-like echidna, give birth to live young and produce milk to feed them. Like all mammals, whales are warm-blooded. This means that their bodies maintain a constant temperature that is usually warmer than their surroundings. To help insulate its organs, the whale has a layer of thick fat, called blubber, just beneath its skin that protects against the loss of heat.

Since mammals need to breathe air, whales must swim to the water's surface regularly. A whale breathes through

its blowhole, a type of nostril located on top of its head. Once it reaches the surface, the whale opens its blowhole, sucks in a great amount of air, and then pinches its blowhole shut as it dives into the water. Toothed whales have one blowhole, and baleen whales have two arranged in a V-shape. Whale muscle has a high concentration of a substance called myoglobin, which helps whales store oxygen in their muscles. This enables them to stay underwater for long periods of time—up to two hours in the case of sperm whales.

When surfacing for air, blue whales breathe three

When a whale opens its blowhole at the surface, it exhales visibly—air comes out in the form of water vapor.

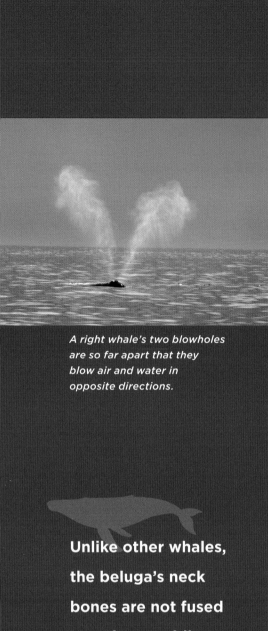

A right whale's two blowholes are so far apart that they blow air and water in opposite directions.

Unlike other whales, the beluga's neck bones are not fused together, enabling belugas to bend their necks and look sideways.

to five times before raising their flukes in the air, a behavior called throwing, and then dive sharply downward. Humpback whales also throw their flukes before a dive, but fin whales rarely do this. A whale's exhaling at the surface, called blowing, also varies by species. The air and mucus that are expelled through the blowhole of the blue whale can reach 30 feet (9 m) above the water and may be visible from a great distance. The sperm whale blows at a forward angle, and the right whale blows two jets that expand like an upside-down pyramid.

Whales have enormous brains. The sperm whale's brain, which weighs about 20 pounds (9 kg), is the largest of any animal's on Earth. Scientists believe that whales are highly intelligent, not because their brains are large but because certain parts of their brains are well developed—particularly the part of the brain responsible for **cognition**. Many whale behaviors suggest that they can learn quickly and understand complex concepts. In fact, whales in captivity have been taught to solve problems and have overcome what appears to be boredom by creating playful activities.

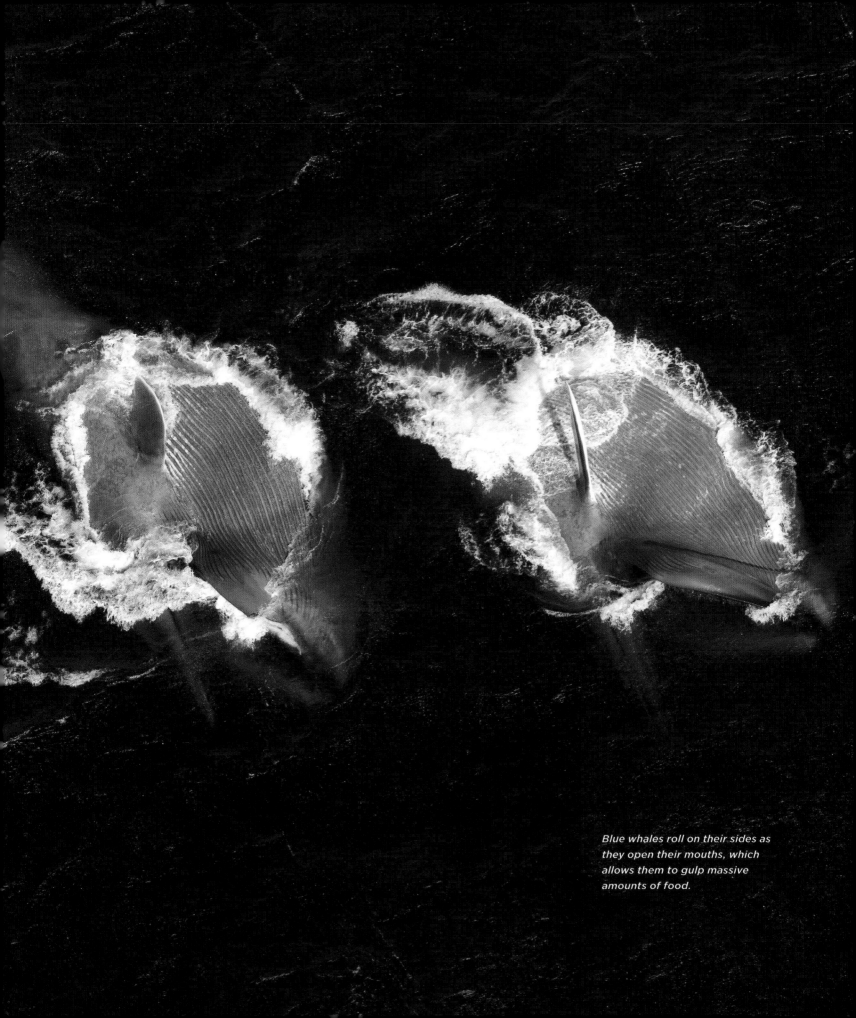

Blue whales roll on their sides as they open their mouths, which allows them to gulp massive amounts of food.

The bond between a whale mother and her calf is one of the strongest of all relationships in the animal kingdom.

WANDERING THE GLOBE

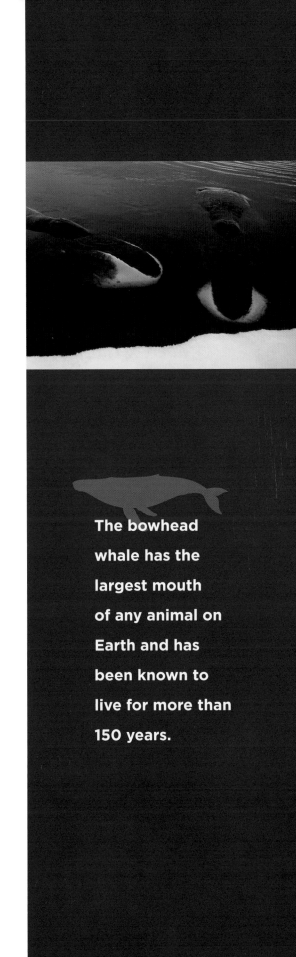

Male whales are called bulls, and females are called cows. Infant whales are called calves. A few whale species, such as minke whales, travel in groups called pods, while most other whales are solitary. Although they generally live alone, this does not mean that whales do not communicate. Baleen whales have folds of tissue in the throat that are used to make true vocalizations that change tone and pitch—like songs—to communicate socially. These sounds are the loudest animal sounds on Earth, and baleen whales can communicate with each other over distances of up to 100 miles (161 km)!

Toothed whales have no folds of tissue to produce sound, so they communicate over short distances by generating clicks, whistles, squeaks, and even deep groans from the blowhole and the **larynx**. Whales use these sounds most often during echolocation, which helps toothed whales to "see" underwater. Baleen whales, such as humpback and blue whales, are grazers, hunting by sight and sound rather than by the vibration of echolocation.

The bowhead whale has the largest mouth of any animal on Earth and has been known to live for more than 150 years.

In 2010, off the coast of South Africa, a whale lured too close by boaters breached and crashed onto the boat.

To echolocate, a toothed whale sends out pulses of sound from various nasal sacs and cavities. These sounds hit objects in their path and bounce back, like echoes, and are captured by a fatty organ in the forehead called a melon. The whale then "reads" the echoes, determining the location, shape, and size of the objects around itself—including prey. The objects can be as big as another whale or as small as a fish. With this ability, whales can locate food, even in total darkness. Whales can also determine the differences between humans and prey animals such as squid and fish. This is the reason, researchers believe, that whales do not attack humans in the open ocean.

Body language is also an important form of communication. Whales of certain species will propel themselves out of the water quickly and fall back down on their side or back with a big splash in a behavior called breaching. This is one way whales show their strength. To attract females or warn off rival males, a male might smack its tail on the water's surface. Whales tell each other where food is located or where danger is lurking by waving a flipper in the air above the water. Some species, such as gray whales and sperm whales,

poke their heads out of the water to look around. This behavior is called spy-hopping.

A spy-hopping whale lifts the front of its head, a beaklike projection called the rostrum, out of the water.

A behavior that is at once predictable yet mysterious is migration. Generation after generation, whales annually travel the same routes from warm-water breeding grounds in the winter to cold-water feeding grounds in the summer and back again. How whales manage to **navigate** these routes, which can cover 3,000 miles (4,828 km) or more, is a mystery, and where they go between these migrations is almost as baffling.

Some scientists believe whales may navigate visually, as they have been observed to spy-hop while traveling

Groups of male humpbacks called competitive pods breach and tail slap to impress females for mating.

parallel to coastlines. It is also believed that whales vocally communicate as they travel in order to stay together on the route. Whales typically spend May to September in cold-water areas feeding on massive gatherings of fish, shrimp, and other small sea creatures. They then travel to warm-water breeding grounds, where they mate and then give birth—a process that lasts about two months during winter or early spring.

While researchers have documented the mating rituals of many whale species, actual breeding is rarely observed. Male humpback whales fighting for the right to breed with a female, an activity called a heat run, was first observed by scientists in 2009. During a heat run, a cow will signal her readiness to breed by slapping the water's surface with her fin and tail and by releasing a scent into the water. After six to eight bulls gather around her, the cow swims away, inviting the males to chase her. They vocalize loudly and blow huge columns of bubbles—displays of aggression that challenge each other to fight over the female. The chase, which often lasts for several hours, can be violent and even deadly, with 40-ton (36 t) bulls crashing into one another and even leaping out of the water to land on competitors.

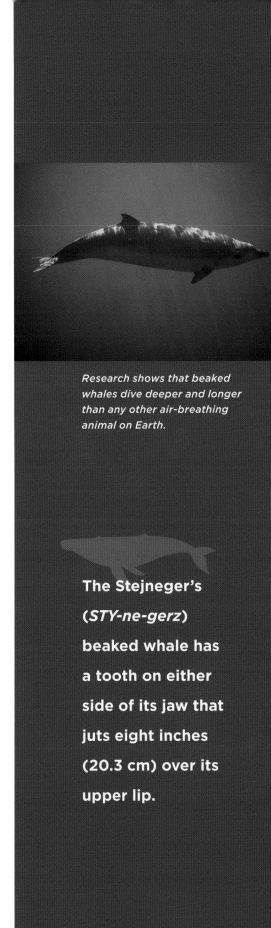

Research shows that beaked whales dive deeper and longer than any other air-breathing animal on Earth.

The Stejneger's (*STY-ne-gerz*) beaked whale has a tooth on either side of its jaw that juts eight inches (20.3 cm) over its upper lip.

The weaker males fall behind as the strongest male follows the female deep into the sea to mate.

Baleen whales have a **gestation** period of about 12 months, but toothed whales, such as sperm whales, can carry their babies for up to 16 months. Usually, only a single calf is born, but sometimes twins occur. When the calf is ready to be born, the mother swims in a twisting, rolling motion to help push out the calf, which emerges tail first so it doesn't drown. Instinct drives the newborn calf toward the water's surface. The mother lifts the calf with her snout to help it take its first breath.

Newborn calves are miniature versions of their parents. Beluga whales are about 5 feet (1.5 m) long at birth, but blue whales can be 23 feet (7 m) long and weigh up to 6,000 pounds (2,721 kg). Calves grow fast and, depending on the species, may gain as much as 200 pounds (91 kg) per day for the first few weeks of their lives. Right whale calves can gain 130 pounds (59 kg) per day, while baby blue whales can gain up to 200 pounds (91 kg) per day. The milk produced by a cow is full of the fat and **nutrients** that her calf needs in order to grow. The calf presses its mouth against teats on its

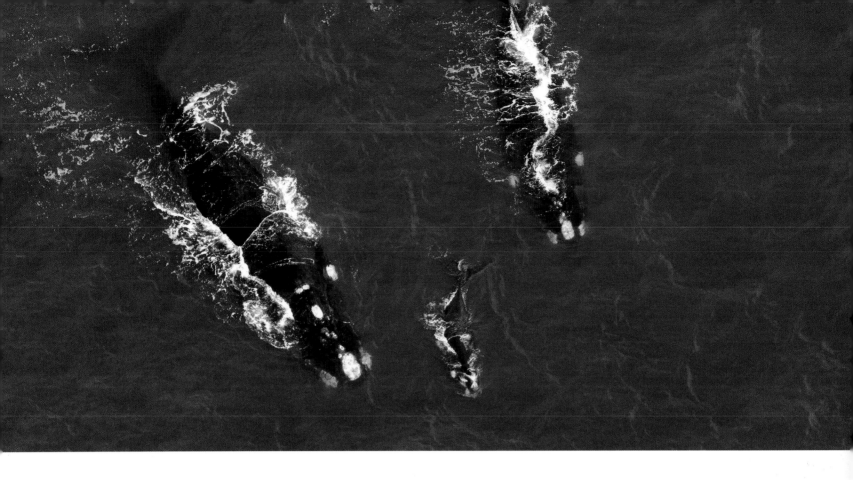

mother's body, and she squirts milk, which is as thick as glue, directly into its mouth.

Despite its large size, a baby whale's life is filled with danger. It is vulnerable to attack by predators such as sharks, and it must make the exhausting journey to the summer feeding grounds with its mother, all the while dependent upon her protection and nourishment. Like most whales, mother blue whales teach their offspring how to feed on krill and small fish by the time they are six months old, but a few species, such as the humpback, may continue to feed their calves milk until the offspring are nearly one year old. Most whale species can live in the wild for 40 to 85 years, but some may live for more than 100 years.

The temporary relationships whales form for the purposes of mating and calving are called "associations."

Early American practices of sperm whaling were described by Herman Melville in his classic 1851 novel Moby-Dick.

A WHALE OF A TALE

Today, people understand that whales are highly intelligent and important to the balance of life in the oceans, but this was not always the case. The practice of whale hunting dates back more than 8,000 years. Whales were at first a necessary food source for coastal people all over the world, but as the centuries passed and civilizations grew, whales became a valuable commodity. **Commercial** whaling from the 17th through the 19th centuries provided bone, baleen, and oil to people in developing cities.

Baleen was used to make flexible materials in the years before plastic was invented. Some baleen objects that were popular in North America included umbrella ribs, women's corsets, bedsprings, and buggy whips. Whale oil, which is actually liquid wax and not true oil, was an equally valuable whale product. It was used for lighting lamps and making candles; later it was used to make machinery run smoothly, which earned it the nickname "train oil." Sperm whales were the most prized species for their oil. While every part of a whale, from its blubber to its bones and muscles, contains oil, a large sperm whale contains as much

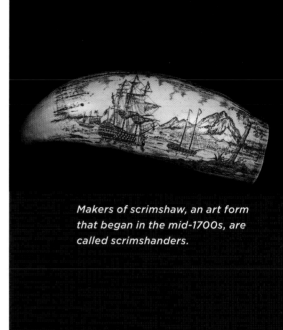

Makers of scrimshaw, an art form that began in the mid-1700s, are called scrimshanders.

The art of scrimshaw was practiced by whalers who carved elaborate images into whalebone, whale teeth, and other materials.

Believed extinct until the 1970s, the western North Pacific gray whale is the rarest on Earth, with fewer than 100 left.

as 6,000 pounds (2,722 kg) of oil in its head cavity alone.

Commercial whaling reached its peak in the early 1900s, with whaling vessels bringing in tens of thousands of whales each year. By the 1920s, though, populations of many whale species had declined drastically from overhunting, with species such as humpback and sperm whales facing extinction. Scientists recognized the problem in the mid-20th century and began traveling with sailors and whalers on their voyages. They soon observed— and helped other people understand—that whales were intelligent animals, valuable for more than just commercial purposes, and organizations in Canada, the United States, and some northern European nations established research projects aimed at learning more about the animals.

In 1986, the International Whaling Commission passed a ban on commercial whaling, making it illegal to hunt whales for purposes other than scientific research. Some nations, including Japan, Norway, and Iceland, have ignored the law, killing more than 25,000 whales since the ban was instated. To hunt and kill whales, modern whaling ships use sophisticated electronic equipment and airplanes that communicate whale sightings to ships. Unlike the wooden harpoons of the early days of whaling, today's harpoons are designed to explode inside a whale, though whales seldom die immediately. Whales have virtually no defense against the machinery of today's whale hunters.

Various species of whale are still hunted for food by certain native peoples of the Arctic, who continue to use traditional tools and methods of hunting. For thousands of years, these **cultures** have valued the whale not only as a food source but also as a symbol of their way of life. Some of the peoples who have made the whale a major part of their **mythologies** include Alaska Native tribes such as the Aleut, Chugach, and Inuit; the Tlingit (*KLING-git*), Kwakwaka'wakw (*KWALK-walk-ya-WALK-wuh*), Haida, and Nuu-cha-nulth peoples of British Columbia; and the Yupik of Russia. Other cultures, including the Vietnamese, believe that whales are divine creatures, like gods, and have a tradition of holding funerals for beached whales.

The Maori people of New Zealand have a strong connection to whales, which act as important spiritual **totems**. One Maori tradition is called whale riding, which is drawn from legends that are unique to individual Maori tribes but tell basically the same story. According to the

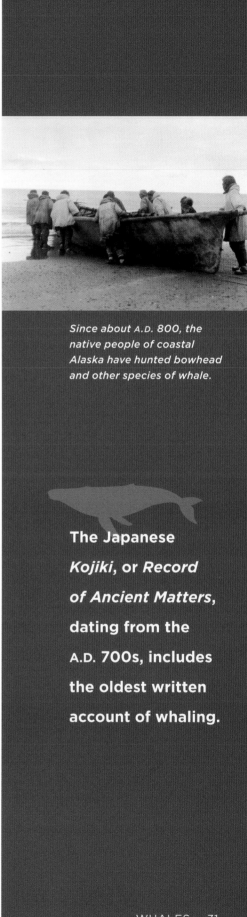

Since about A.D. 800, the native people of coastal Alaska have hunted bowhead and other species of whale.

The Japanese *Kojiki*, or *Record of Ancient Matters*, dating from the A.D. 700s, includes the oldest written account of whaling.

WHALES WEEP NOT!

They say the sea is cold, but the sea contains
the hottest blood of all, and the wildest, the most urgent.

All the whales in the wider deeps, hot are they, as they urge
on and on, and dive beneath the icebergs.
The right whales, the sperm-whales, the hammer-heads, the killers
there they blow, there they blow, hot wild white breath out of
    the sea! . . . .

And enormous mother whales lie dreaming suckling their whale-
tender young
and dreaming with strange whale eyes wide open in the waters of
    the beginning and the end.

And bull-whales gather their women and whale-calves in a ring
when danger threatens, on the surface of the ceaseless flood
and range themselves like great fierce Seraphim facing the threat
encircling their huddled monsters of love.
And all this happens in the sea, in the salt
where God is also love, but without words:
and Aphrodite is the wife of whales
most happy, happy she!

by D. H. Lawrence (1885–1930)

Ngati Porou tribe, Paikea, a man from a faraway place, was invited on a fishing trip with his brother Ruatapu and some other men. Ruatapu, who was jealous of Paikea, sank his brother's canoe in a plan to drown him. But Paikea called on the *taniwha*, or spirits of the sea, for help. A spirit in the form of a whale carried Paikea to the shore of *Aotearoa*, known today as New Zealand, where he established his tribe and became a great chief. This story was the basis for the 2002 film *Whale Rider*, which features a modern Maori girl attempting to ride a southern right whale to prove her potential to become the first female leader of her tribe.

Two humpback whales were featured in the 1986 film *Star Trek IV: The Voyage Home*. In the movie's setting of the 23rd century, whales have been hunted to extinction. Captain James Kirk and his crew travel back to the 20th century to retrieve a pair of humpback whales in order to repopulate the species on the Earth of the future. Farther back in movie history, an enormous whale was featured in the 1940 Walt Disney Pictures release *Pinocchio*. A giant whale named Monstro swallows Pinocchio's father, Geppetto, but Pinocchio saves his father by setting a fire in the whale's belly, causing the whale to sneeze them out.

Film critics such as Roger Ebert consider Pinocchio's escape from Monstro to be one of the greatest scenes in any Disney movie.

Second only to the blue whale in length and able to swim 30 miles (48 km) per hour, the fin whale is called the "greyhound of the sea."

The film is based on *The Adventures of Pinocchio*, written by Carlo Collodi from 1881 to 1883.

The story of Geppetto and the whale may have had its roots in the ancient story of Jonah and the whale, which is found in three religious books—the Hebrew Bible, the Christian Old Testament, and the Muslim Qur'an. Another literary whale can be found in the 1851 novel *Moby-Dick* by Herman Melville, which features an enormous sperm whale that destroys the whaling ship *Pequod* and its vengeful captain, Ahab. This novel may have been inspired by the true experience of the whaler *Essex*, which sank after being rammed by a sperm whale in 1820. A year later, whale hunter Owen Chase, one of only eight survivors, wrote a nonfiction account of the ordeal.

Whales do not typically attack boats; in fact, most whales are gentle, nonthreatening creatures that approach boats and people only out of curiosity. To get closer to whales, people go on whale-watching tours. This practice of commercial whale watching began in 1971 with the Zoological Society of Montreal's field trips down the St. Lawrence River to view beluga and fin whales. Since then, whale watching has become a multimillion-dollar

enterprise around the world. In Brazil, visitors can take boats offshore to view humpback whales, and off the New England coast of the U.S., fin, minke, and endangered North Atlantic right whales can be seen. Sperm whales are common in New Zealand, and southern right whales swim near the shores of South Africa.

In Hawaii, researchers who study humpback whale diving hope to better understand the whales' nighttime behavior.

Cetologists study dolphins such as pilot whales—which, despite their name, are not true whales—as well.

GIANTS OF THE SEA

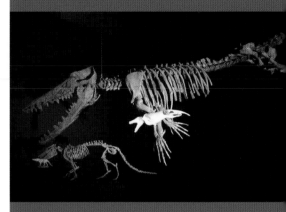

Ambulocetus *is nicknamed "the walking whale" because it could walk on land as well as swim in the sea.*

Millions of years ago, whale ancestors lived on land. Scientists believe that whales **evolved** from four-legged mammals that lived in and around streams and shallow lakes and ate vegetation. One such creature was the 10-foot-long (3 m) *Ambulocetus*, which lived about 50 million years ago. Its body resembled an otter's, but its head and long snout looked like a crocodile's. It had teeth like a modern killer whale and hunted fish and small animals both on land and in the water.

As these prehistoric mammals began to spend more time in the water, they lost their legs, gaining webbed limbs and eventually flippers instead. Over many millions of years, these creatures grew very large, out-competing any other predators. They gradually became more torpedo-shaped and developed the dorsal fin. Fossil research indicates that primitive baleen whales began using their unique method of feeding 20 to 30 million years ago, and toothed whales started developing the ability to echolocate 10 million years ago.

The wide variety of modern whales and their relatives makes cetology, or the study of cetaceans, a far-reaching field of study. The American Cetacean Society sponsors research that aims to answer numerous questions about whales, such as how **global warming** affects them, how sperm whales catch squid, why whales beach themselves, and how human-created noise in the ocean may affect humpback whale communication. This last subject is part of a larger area of study—that of the relationship between communication and culture. Whale scientists, called cetologists, believe that both the variation and repetition of whale songs is evidence that whales have cultures, which can vary from place to place and change over time.

The first cetologist to record whale sounds was William Schevill of the Woods Hole Oceanographic Institution in Massachusetts. In the 1950s, Schevill dropped a **hydrophone** connected to a long cable into the sea and listened to the sounds made by blue and sperm whales, as well as other marine mammals. In 1967, biologist Roger Payne began to specifically study the sounds made by humpback whales. He determined that the sounds were actually songs that had repeated patterns and rhythms. From that time on, scientists have been fascinated by the mystery of whale songs.

Research conducted by Canada's Dalhousie University in 2002 revealed that sperm whales in various locations around the globe have their own vocal language variations, or dialects, that are passed down from the older whales to the calves. Scientists believe that dialects indicate a whale's association with a particular group—a function of dialects in human language as well. Some groups travel extensively, while others remain in certain general areas, but each group is a distinct culture—with its own language. Also, in a given year, humpback whales as far apart as Hawaii and Mexico have been found to

Researchers can get close to whales because the animals tend to be placid and tolerant, like big cows.

In recent years, cruise ships have struck and killed whales in greater numbers, including humpback and fin whales along Canada's coast.

sing identical songs, an act that has scientists baffled. More incredible is the fact that as the songs change from year to year, the groups of whales, which are vastly far apart geographically, all change their songs at the same time.

In 2000, many scientists around the world concluded that noise in the ocean—from ships and industry— is having a profound effect on whales. Research suggests that a variety of sources adversely affect whale communication: cargo and cruise ships running huge engines; commercial fishing vessels using electronic fish locaters; military use of sonar, or sound waves, to detect underwater objects; and incredibly loud seismic air guns, which release massive bursts of high-pressure air into the water to map oil and gas deposits under the ocean floor. Researchers believe that such noise may interfere with whales' navigation abilities, causing them to stray from migration routes and even beach themselves on shorelines.

While a number of large-scale international organizations conduct general whale research, many other, smaller groups concentrate on particular species. The Hawaii Whale Research Foundation focuses on humpback whales, the New England Aquarium targets right whale topics, and the Minke Whale Project in Queensland, Australia, specializes in the study of dwarf minke whales. Typical of whale tracking projects, a study of beluga whales in Bristol Bay, Alaska, involves capturing the whales, taking from them small samples of blood and blubber, and fitting them with **Global Positioning System** (GPS) tracking devices. Called a "spider tag," the device is a small rectangular box with six "legs" that are buried harmlessly in the whale's thick blubber. The spider tag sends an electronic signal that is picked up by a weather satellite. The data that is gathered helps researchers track whale movement—valuable information that can be used in efforts to conserve dwindling populations.

Scientists have named one dwarf minke whale song the "Star Wars sound" for its resemblance to a science-fiction laser gun.

Research projects such as these increase public awareness of the plight of whales, leading to intensified conservation efforts. A 10-year study of South Pacific humpback whales conducted by the Center for Cetacean Research & Conservation led to the establishment of a 386,000-square-mile (999,735 sq km) whale sanctuary in the Cook Islands. Whales need protected areas due to the threats still posed by **poachers**.

One whale that has been carefully monitored in efforts to protect him from whale hunters is Migaloo, the world's only all-white humpback whale. His name means "white fella" in a native language of Australia. He was first spotted off Australia's east coast in 1991 and has since been tracked nearly every year along his migration route. Migaloo is part of a group of humpback whales that feed in Antarctica during the summer and migrate to the warm waters of Australia's Great Barrier Reef in winter. The Pacific Whale Foundation, the group that monitors Migaloo, is concerned for the white whale's safety from whale hunters, as his bright coloring makes him an easy target. Authorities in Australia passed a law making it illegal for anyone to come within 1,640 feet (500 m) of

Migaloo while he is in Australian waters, but he is not protected from poachers when he is in the open sea.

Being ocean-dwelling animals, whales are difficult to study. Enough has been learned about them to spark public concern for their conservation, but much more information is needed. With further education, stronger international laws, and more financial support, organizations around the world can continue to help whales survive on this ever-changing planet.

Visitors to www.migaloo.com.au can keep up to date on sightings of Migaloo and other members of his pod.

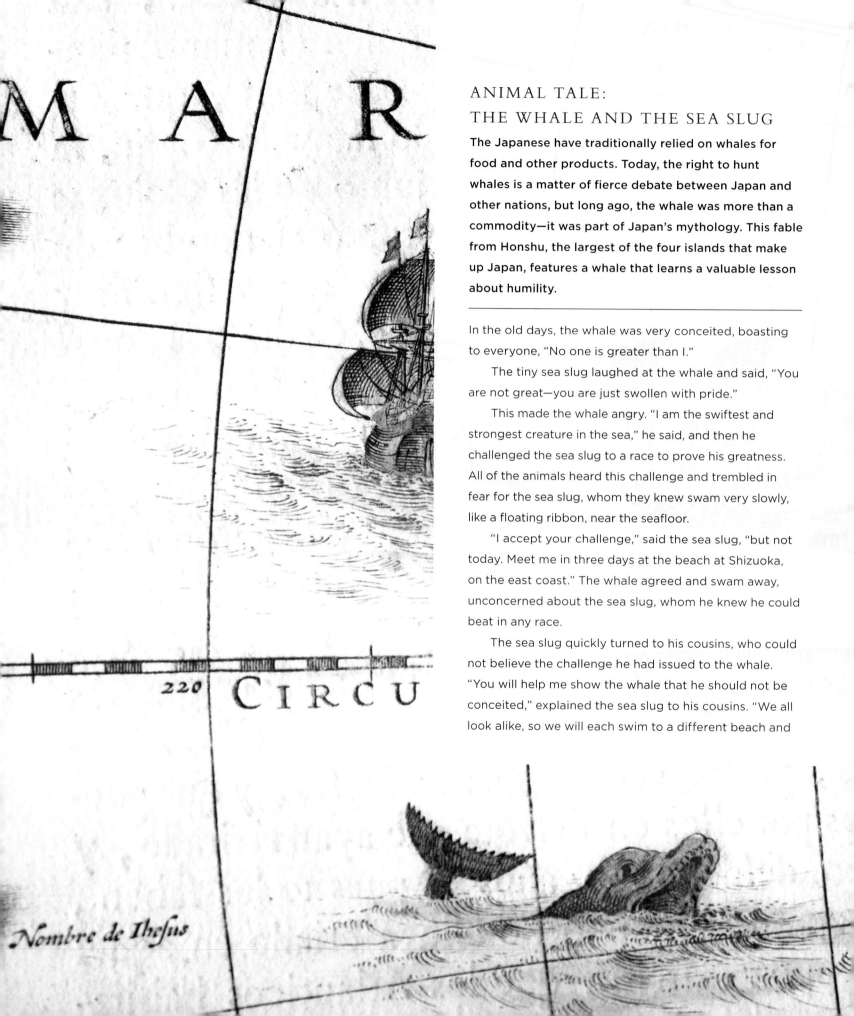

ANIMAL TALE:
THE WHALE AND THE SEA SLUG

The Japanese have traditionally relied on whales for food and other products. Today, the right to hunt whales is a matter of fierce debate between Japan and other nations, but long ago, the whale was more than a commodity—it was part of Japan's mythology. This fable from Honshu, the largest of the four islands that make up Japan, features a whale that learns a valuable lesson about humility.

In the old days, the whale was very conceited, boasting to everyone, "No one is greater than I."

The tiny sea slug laughed at the whale and said, "You are not great—you are just swollen with pride."

This made the whale angry. "I am the swiftest and strongest creature in the sea," he said, and then he challenged the sea slug to a race to prove his greatness. All of the animals heard this challenge and trembled in fear for the sea slug, whom they knew swam very slowly, like a floating ribbon, near the seafloor.

"I accept your challenge," said the sea slug, "but not today. Meet me in three days at the beach at Shizuoka, on the east coast." The whale agreed and swam away, unconcerned about the sea slug, whom he knew he could beat in any race.

The sea slug quickly turned to his cousins, who could not believe the challenge he had issued to the whale. "You will help me show the whale that he should not be conceited," explained the sea slug to his cousins. "We all look alike, so we will each swim to a different beach and trick the whale." The sea slug's cousins agreed, and they all set off in different directions.

The day of the race came, and the whale and the sea slug agreed to race northeast along the coast to Sendai. The whale arrived in no time, but when he approached the beach, he was met by the sea slug's cousin, whom he could not tell apart from the first sea slug. "What took you so long?" said the sea slug. "Perhaps we should race again."

They agreed to race around the north side of the island to Niigata on the west coast. Off they went, with the whale swimming far ahead. But when the whale reached Niigata, there was another of the sea slug's cousins. "What took you so long?" the sea slug asked the whale, who was starting to feel embarrassed.

"Let us race around the south side of the island back to Shizuoka," said the whale. "It is such a long way that I will most certainly beat you." The sea slug agreed, and the whale rushed back out to sea.

At the beach at Shizuoka, the sea slug was waiting for the whale, who had no idea he had been tricked. "You are not the greatest creature in the sea," declared the sea slug. "You are no more important than all the other creatures in the sea—we all work together in our ocean world."

"You are right," admitted the whale. "I was wrong to be so conceited. Little sea slugs are just as important as mighty whales. Everyone is equal." And with that, the whale went back out to sea feeling a little bit smaller in a world that felt a little bit bigger.

GLOSSARY

camouflage – the ability to hide, due to coloring or markings that blend in with a given environment

cognition – the mental process of gaining understanding through experience, thought, and the senses

commercial – used for business and to gain a profit rather than for personal reasons

cultures – particular groups in a society that share behaviors and characteristics that are accepted as normal by that group

evolved – gradually developed into a new form

extinct – having no living members

gestation – the period of time it takes a baby to develop inside its mother's womb

Global Positioning System – a system of satellites, computers, and other electronic devices that work together to determine the location of objects or living things that carry a trackable device

global warming – the gradual increase in Earth's temperature that causes changes in climates, or long-term weather conditions, around the world

hydrophone – a device designed for detecting and amplifying underwater sounds

larynx – the organ in the neck of mammals that protects the throat and houses the vocal cords (when present)

mythologies – collections of myths, or popular, traditional beliefs or stories that explain how something came to be or that are associated with a person or object

navigate – to plan and follow a course of travel

nutrients – substances that give an animal energy and help it grow

plankton – microscopic algae and animals that drift or float in the ocean

poachers – people who hunt protected species of wild animals, even though doing so is against the law

resistance – the slowing effect applied by one thing against another

totems – objects, animals, or plants respected as symbols of a tribe and often used in ceremonies and rituals

SELECTED BIBLIOGRAPHY

Bortolotti, Dan. *Wild Blue: A Natural History of the World's Largest Animal*. New York: Thomas Dunne Books, 2008.

Chadwick, Douglas H. *The Grandest of Lives: Eye to Eye with Whales*. San Francisco: Sierra Club Books, 2006.

Greenpeace International. "Whale Factsheets." http://www.greenpeace.org/international/campaigns/oceans/whaling/whale-factsheets.

Kelsey, Ellen. *Watching Giants: The Secret Lives of Whales*. Berkeley: University of California Press, 2009.

Save the Whales. "Homepage." http://www.savethewhales.org.

Thompson, Doug. *Whales: Touching the Mystery*. Troutdale, Ore.: NewSage Press, 2006.